This book belongs to:

_____

This book is dedicated to my grandmother, Deborah Sistrunk - Nelson. I also want to dedicate this to my late Uncle Chub aka Anthony Caldwell Jr.

Special thanks to my mother, Winnie Caldwell and the entire Books N Bros community for supporting me.

Cool Bros Read

Written by Sidney Keys III
Illustrated by Afzal Khan
Editor: Winnie Caldwell
Writing Coach: Arriel Biggs

Copyright © 2020 by Books N Bros ®
All Rights Reserved. This book or any portion thereof may not be reproduced or used in any manner whatsoever without the express written permission of the publisher except for the use of brief quotations in a book review.
Printed in the United States of America
ISBN: 978-0-578-87265-0

Books all around as I sit on my granny's lap, reading books of adventure.
She's helped me to believe Cool Bros Read.

As I travel time with new adventures in my mind, I open a new book and it speaks to me. The book also speaks to the new person I could be, And I'm reminded Cool Bros Read.

As I walk in the store₁, on the floor, I'm surrounded by books of children who look like me. And after going viral on social media, for reading these stories, I am even more inspired that Cool Bros Read.

As a young boy, I have always loved to read. Although, I couldn't find books that looked like me. It was time to do my part so I made a book club as a start. Through Books N Bros$_2$ I am teaching my bros to get (Lit)erature$_3$ because why?
Cool Bros Read!

Flying state to state[4] with my mom to inspire, while the community helps us build an empire. So we can show the world in fact, that Cool Bros Read.

As I talk to my peers, they don't want to read, They cannot see what is hidden within a good mystery. I tell them my story and motivate them to believe Cool Bros Read.

As I grow older and my head reaches my Uncle Chub's shoulders, he reminds me to give back and help the community when there is a need. And of course to remember, Cool Bros Read

Now I have built friendships through books, created a brotherhood of Bros who believe you must read in order to succeed.

Our favorite series 'Scraps of Time' was flowing throughout our minds while we traveled in the stands of the Negro League.

We listened to jazz during the Harlem Renaissance. And thanks to the late great, Patricia C. McKissack[6], now we understand the importance of why Cool Bros Read!

After finding my voice in 2016, we have established why cool bros read. With stories from great black and brown people of the past, present, and future, we control what's next!
Remember to strive to be your best!
And never forget Cool Bros Read.

About the author

Sidney Keys III is a St. Louis, MO, 15 year-old native and rising entrepreneur, who decided to take his love for reading to the next level and create Books n Bros at the young age of 10! Having multiple meet ups with different boys, ages 7-13 years old, as a way to advocate for African American literacy, he is paving the way for change.

You may recognize him from appearances like: Oprah's magazine, The Steve Harvey Show, Good Morning America, Cartoon Network, CNN, Huffington Post or on Disney+ as a MARVEL Hero!

His goal when he grows up is to be an even larger entrepreneur than what he is now, to partner with schools and be an example for future young leaders.

He wants to continue to be a philanthropist and give back to the community, and looking at attending an HBCU when it's time for college for African American studies!

Inspiration:

Pictured from left to right, Sidney's grandma Deborah, Sidney, and his late Grandpa Dirk.

Sidney reading in his elementary school's library at Russell Elementary in Hazelwood, MO. Photo credit: CNN

Sidney at 10 years old, the first time he visited an African American Bookstore ever!

Sidney at 14 years old during the 2020 Juneteenth celebration in St. Louis, MO. Photo by: Richard B. Washinton

Inspiration:

Photo from Books N Bros meetup with members reading with 'Big Bro', volunteer, Ishmael Sistrunk (also Sidney's uncle!)

Sidney and his mom traveling the U.S.!

Sidney at the 2019 Black Excellence in Literature, the first gala Books N Bros hosted!

Pictured left to right: Marjorie Harvey, Winnie Caldwell, Sidney Keys III and Steve Harvey at SteveTV in LA December 2017!

Index/Important References

1. References to Sidney's first visit to the only African American children's book store in St. Louis, MO! Visit http://bit.ly/sidneystorevisit to see the viral footage!

2. Books N Bros is the first National subscription book club of its kind! Founded in 2016, Sidney and his mother Winnie created Books N Bros; a subscription based book club for boys to bring awareness to African American literacy!

3. Want to get (lit)erature? See the custom hoodies created by Sidney in his shop! Booksnbros.com/shop

4. Since it's inception, Sidney has traveled from St. Louis to New York, California, Ohio, Georgia and his mom even travelled to speak to moms in Canada about Books N Bros!

5. Sidney's late uncle, Anthony Ray Caldwell Jr was deemed as special needs as a child but in fact tested as gifted! Instead of being placed in advanced classes, Chub was bored in the classroom and unfortunately isn't living today due to street violence. Sidney's mom didn't want that to be the story of any of the bros, so she founded the non-profit Chub Cares Adopt A Bro, to give the same services of Books N Bros to families in need completely for free. See more at adopt.booksnbros.com

6. Patricia C. McKissack is a legendary author and was also a native of St. Louis, MO! Sidney and the bros enjoyed her Scraps Of Time series so much, they read all of the books! We lift up her name forever.

Questions for the classroom

1. Where has Sidney lived?

2. What age range are the boys for Books N Bros?
(Extra Credit: What was the original age range and why?)

3. Who is Patricia C. McKissack?

4. What is the name of the bookstore that Sidney visited and went viral on social media?

5. What type of college does Sidney want to attend?

6. Is Sidney's book club only for one race?

7. Why is a book club like Books N Bros important?

8. What is Sidney's super hero name?

9. What is Sidney's signature hair cut?

10. How old was Sidney when he started Books N Bros?

11. What will you do to advocate for your peers and community?

Answers

1. **Where has Sidney lived?** St. Louis, MO and Atlanta, GA

2. **What age range are the boys for Books N Bros? (Extra Credit: What was the original age range and why?)** 7-13, originally 8-12, because statistically boys ages 8-12 don't score as well as others and he wants to combat that.

3. **Who is Patricia C. McKissack?** Patricia C. and Fredrick L. McKissack have written over one hundred books about the African-American experience. They have won countless awards and received much critical acclaim, all the while bringing enjoyment and information to young readers.
Before becoming a full-time writer, Patricia worked as a teacher and then as an editor of children's books. "My career as a teacher helped me recognize what books were needed and what children enjoyed reading; my career as an editor taught me how to develop an idea. After teaching for nine years and editing for six, I felt I was ready to launch my writing career. Fred worked first as a civil engineer for the city of St. Louis and the U.S. Army, and later owned his own general contracting company in St. Louis. Now he devotes his time to the family business, All-Writing Services.

4. **What is the name of the bookstore that Sidney visited and went viral on social media?** EyeSeeMe African American Children's Bookstore

5. **What type of college does Sidney want to attend?** An HBCU (Historically Black College or University)

6. **Is Sidney's book club only for one race?** Books N Bros is for ALL boys who want to learn more about African American stories in a cool, positive way!

7. **Why is a book club like Books N Bros important?** Freebie! Your answers only matter here :)

8. **What is Sidney's super hero name?** The Spectacular Sidney

9. **What is Sidney's signature hair cut?** A box style hair cut with a low fade on the sides and back!

10. **How old was Sidney when he started Books N Bros?** 10 years old!

11. **What will you do to advocate for your peers and community?** We are waiting for your answer! The world is yours!

*Feel free to share your worksheets with us on social! Facebook/Twitter/Instagram: @booksnbros

www.ingramcontent.com/pod-product-compliance
Lightning Source LLC
LaVergne TN
LVHW072101070426
835508LV00002B/216